G000136394

Purple Ronnie's Little Guide to

MEN

by Purple Ronnie

First published 1999 by Boxtree
an imprint of PanMacmillan Publishers Ltd.
20 New Wharf Road
London N1 9RR

www.macmillan.com

Associated companies throughout the world

ISBN 0 7522 7240 3

9 8 7 6 5 4

A CIP catalogue record for this book is
available from the British Library

Text by Giles Andreae
Illustrations by Janet Cronin
Printed and Bound in Hong Kong

Arty Men

floaty hair →

posy chin fluff →

← girly shirt

pee poems

a poem about

Arty Men

Arty Men like to be
different
To show how creative
they are
So don't be surprised
If they butter their
thighs
And start barking out
loud at your car

An Arty Man's brain is on
a completely different
planet to everyone else's

Macho Men

a poem about

Macho Men

Some men think it's cool
to bare

A bulging chest with
loads of hair

But if you talk to one
you'll find

His brains are stuck
up his behind

is there anyone in there?
knock knock
waffle...blah ...swank... rubbish
← talking out of bum

Sometimes it can be difficult to find a Macho Man's doodah because there are so many muscles in the way

Mummy's Boys

nice parting
chubby cheeks
favourite teddy
Mummy's sarnies
clean pants

a poem about
↓

Mummy's Boys

When you date a Mummy's
Boy

They always bring their
Mums

Then sit there cuddling
their shawls

And sucking on their
thumbs

Mummy's Boys' clothes ar
incredibly tidy, they have
creases in everything
and they always smell of
roses

Lager Lads

OY! wot you starin' at?
meat head
BOLLOCKS
spotty bum
England pants

a poem about

Lager Lads

Lager Lads love going
out with their mates

In fact it's their favourite
trick

To gobble down masses of
curry and beer

And pass out in piles of
sick

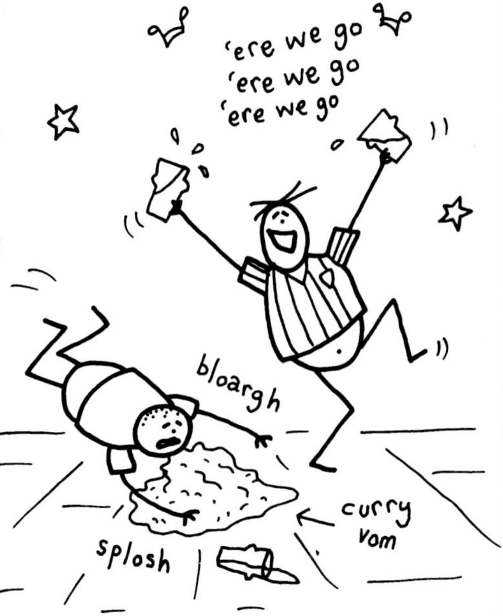
'ere we go
'ere we go
'ere we go
bloargh
curry
vom
splosh

A Lager Lad's favourite joke is showing his bottom to people

a poem about ↓

Weeds

Some men think weeds
are pathetic
Because they're so fussy
and neat
But most people find
That they're friendly and kind
And girls always say that
they're sweet

Grown-up weeds have two straggly hairs on their chests which they are very proud of

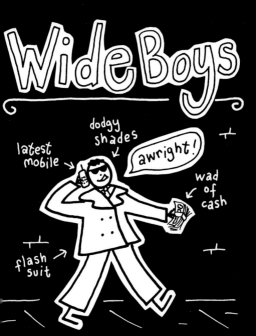

a poem about ↓

Wide Boys

They're always on their
mobile phones
Cutting dodgy deals
Looking sharp in shiny
suits
And nifty sets of wheels

i'll do the fluffy bears at twenty quid and the wind-up grannies at fifty
speed

A Wide Boy will love you
forever if you let him
Do It with you in the
back of his car

a poem about
Girly Men

Girly Men think playing
sport is too rough
So they love to go shopping
instead
And when they get home
They spend hours on the
phone
Before wearing their face
masks to bed

Girly Men's bathrooms are stuffed full of all sorts of lotions and potions for making themselves feel gorgeous

a poem about

Slobs

They walk around in clouds
of smoke

They splutter burp and
wheeze

They live off mouldy
sausages

And whiff of rancid
cheese

A slob's favourite kind of date is to have a cosy dinner for two at home

a poem about a

Sport Man

No girl can get close
to a Sport Man
Without passing out on
the spot
The air in his room
Has the subtle perfume
Of the sweat on a
wrestler's bot

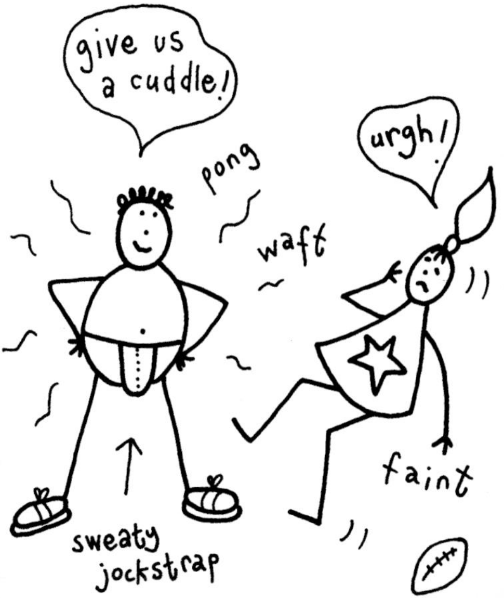
give us a cuddle!
pong
urgh!
waft
faint
sweaty jockstrap

Sport Men like nothing better than spending the whole weekend shouting at the T.V.

Gadget Men

pasty face

loads of kit

crucial new game

DEATH Zombie 4

ELECTRIC HEAVEN

radioactive

a poem about ↓

Gadget Men

A Gadget Man will never be

The lover of your dreams

Cos the only things that turn them on

Are groovy new machines

v. bored
rubbish boyfriend
do you like spam sandwiches?
sums lists
.com dinner
buzz
ring ring
tap tap

Gadget Men speak in a
language that only other
Gadget Men can understan

a poem about a
Perfect Man

Most girls want a man
who is perfect
But maybe not many exist
Who've got charm and
panache
Several sackloads of
cash
And a willy the size of
your wrist

how big's your thingie?
are you single?
how much is in here?
rifle

Perfect Men know exactly
where to touch you and
they can keep going all
night long